Oraciones para ir a dormir,

dar las gracias y compartir

Oraciones para ir a dormir, dar las gracias y compartir

Ana Galán

Ilustrado por Núria Feijoó

everest

Rezar es hablar con Dios,
aquí o en cualquier lugar,
en el coche, en la cama
o en mitad del alta mar.

Rezar es hablar con Dios,
en voz alta o callado,
ojos cerrados o abiertos,
sentado o arrodillado.

Rezar no es solo pedir.
Es dar gracias, compartir.
Es contar tus alegrías,
tus tristezas y tus iras.

Para *rezar* no hay normas
ni edades ni obligaciones,
puedes decir lo que piensas
o recitar oraciones.

Rezar es hablar con Dios,
porque es un buen amigo,
porque Él siempre te escucha,
porque siempre está contigo.

Oraciones para ir a dormir

Cuatro esquinitas

Cuatro esquinitas tiene mi cama.
Cuatro angelitos que me la guardan.
Dos a los pies,
dos a la cabecera
y la Virgen María que es mi compañera.

Jesusito de mi vida

Jesusito de mi vida,
eres niño como yo
y por eso te quiero tanto
y te doy mi corazón.

Ángel de la guarda

Ángel de la guarda,
dulce compañía,
no me desampares
ni de noche ni de día.

Las horas que pasan,
las horas del día,
si tú estás conmigo,
serán de alegría.

No me dejes solo,
sé en todo mi guía;
sin ti soy chiquito
y me perdería.

Ven siempre a mi lado,
tu mano en la mía.
Ángel de la guarda,
dulce compañía.

Me ha contado Jesusito,
viene para que yo sea
un angelito en el cielo
y su amigo aquí en la Tierra.

Yo le he dicho a Jesusito
que yo seré aquí en la Tierra
su amiguito para siempre
y que en el cielo le vea.

Señor Jesucristo
que bendices tu altar,
bendice mi cama
que me voy a acostar.

Méceme, Virgen María,
quiero dormirme en tus brazos,
guárdame, oh Madre mía,
con Jesús en tu regazo.

13

Buenas noches, Jesusito,
ayúdame a dormir bien,
a mi papá y a mi mamá
y a mis hermanos también.

Amén, Jesús,
a meternos en la cama
y a apagar la luz.

Con Dios me acuesto,
con Dios me levanto,
con la Virgen María
y el Espíritu Santo.

Oraciones para dar las gracias

Gracias, Jesús,
por crear los mares,
las plantas, el cielo
y los animales.
Gracias por mi familia.
Gracias por los amigos.
Gracias porque yo sé
que siempre estarás conmigo.

Bendita la luz del día

Bendita la luz del día
y el Señor que nos la envía.
¡Bendito el Niño Jesús,
bendita Santa María!

Gracias, Dios, por no dármelo todo,
sino solo lo que necesito.

20

Para que te encuentres cómodo,
Señor, en mi habitación,
voy a ordenarlo todo
y también mi corazón.

Te ofrezco, Señor, mi trabajo
como ofrenda limpia y pura,
mi esfuerzo desde aquí abajo
hasta ti quiero que suba.

Gracias, Señor, por tu casa,
porque tú siempre me invitas.
Como siempre, este domingo
iré a hacerte una visita.

23

Oraciones para pedir perdón

Perdón, Señor, por mis pecados
que me separan de ti,
pues para siempre a tu lado
contigo quiero vivir.

Hoy, Jesús, estoy muy triste
porque me porté muy mal.
Perdona por lo que hice.
Ayúdame a no hacerlo más.

Perdona cuando me enfado
o no quiero compartir.
Perdona cuando soy vago
y a mamá le hago sufrir.
Perdona si no me esfuerzo
y a veces digo mentiras.
Perdona si no te ayudo
siempre que me lo pidas.

Jesús, que en el Sagrario
te encuentras prisionero,
mi corazón te ofrezco
lleno de amor sincero.

Perdona mis pecados,
mira que soy tu amigo.
Abre por favor la puerta
que quiero vivir contigo.

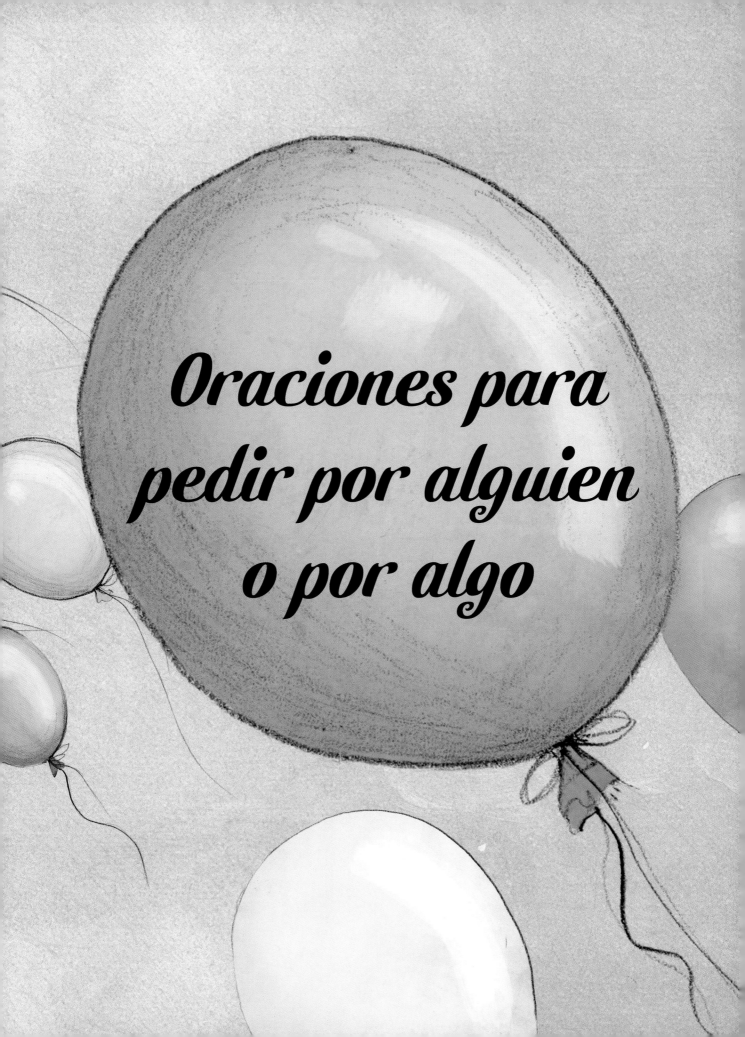

Oraciones para pedir por alguien o por algo

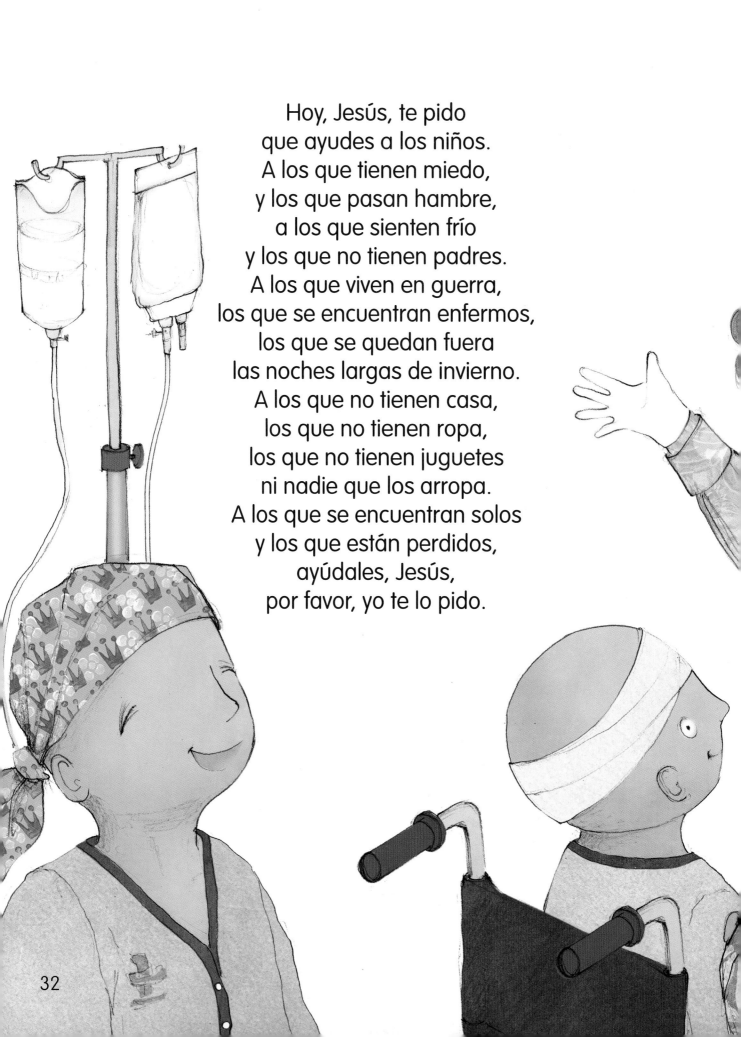

Hoy, Jesús, te pido
que ayudes a los niños.
A los que tienen miedo,
y los que pasan hambre,
a los que sienten frío
y los que no tienen padres.
A los que viven en guerra,
los que se encuentran enfermos,
los que se quedan fuera
las noches largas de invierno.
A los que no tienen casa,
los que no tienen ropa,
los que no tienen juguetes
ni nadie que los arropa.
A los que se encuentran solos
y los que están perdidos,
ayúdales, Jesús,
por favor, yo te lo pido.

Niñito Jesús,
yo quiero ser bueno.
Ayúdame tú
que solito no puedo.

En mi corazón de niño
guardo yo muchos deseos,
el primero es que los hombres
sean cada vez más buenos.

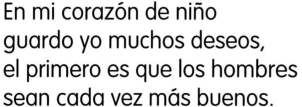

El segundo es que la gente
viva siempre en armonía,
y que esté siempre contenta
con el pan de cada día.

Yo pido por mis padres
y los padres de otros niños,
para que nunca se separen
y que siempre estén unidos.

Haz que no exista la guerra,
ni tan siquiera en los libros,
y en el mundo en que estamos
no se oiga llorar a un niño.
Así sea.
Amén.

Tú, Señor, que fuiste niño
y que siempre me acompañas,
a ti, que nunca me engañas
y me tratas con cariño,
te ofrezco mis pocos años,
te ofrezco mis muchos sueños,
líbrame de todo daño,
porque tú eres mi Dueño.

La oración del abecedario

Enséñame, Jesús,

a *a*yudar

y ser *b*ueno.

Ayúdame a *c*ompartir

y repartir mi *d*inero.

Enséñame a *e*scuchar,

a hacer muchos *f*avores,

a guiar, a dar las *g*racias,

y no *h*erir a los mayores.

Ayúdame a no *i*nsultar,

a *j*ugar sin pelear,

a recorrer *k*ilómetros

y por la gente *l*uchar.

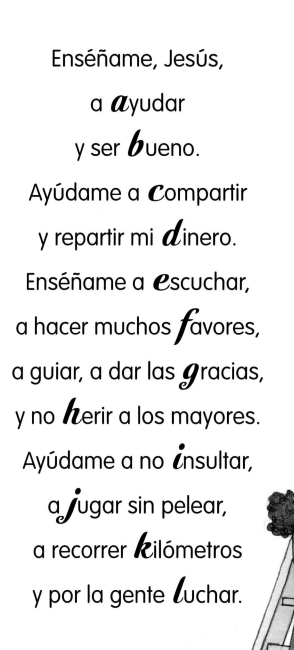

Enséñame a no **m**olestar
o pedir sin **n**ecesidad.
Enséñame a **o**lvidar
y perdonar con **p**iedad.
Ayúdame a **q**uerer,
a **r**espetar al mundo entero,
a **s**aber, a **s**ervir
y **t**rabajar con esmero.
Ayúdame a ser **ú**til,
a solo decir la **v**erdad,
a incluir a Ana o **W**ill
y no e**x**cluir a los demás.
A**y**údame, Jesús, a vivir
y contigo ser feli**z**.

Oraciones para bendecir la mesa

Bendice Señor los alimentos
que vamos a tomar.
Amén.

Hoy, Jesús, pongo la mesa
para ti y con amor.
Para que estemos unidos
y todo sepa mejor.

Bendícenos, Señor, y bendice nuestros alimentos.
Bendice también a quienes nos los han preparado
y da pan a los que no lo tienen.

Bendito seas, Señor, Dios del universo,
por estos alimentos,
fruto de la tierra y del trabajo del hombre,
que hemos recibido de tu bondad
y ahora vamos a compartir.
Amén.

El Niño Jesús que nació en Belén
bendiga estos alimentos y a nosotros también.

Bendice, Señor, a cuantos
hoy comemos este pan.
Bendice a quienes lo hicieron,
a quienes no lo tendrán.
Haz que juntos lo comamos
en la Mesa Celestial.

Gracias te damos, Señor,
por el pan que nos mantiene,
otorga por más favor
el darlo a quien no lo tiene.

Padrenuestro

Padre nuestro, que estás en el cielo,
santificado sea tu nombre,
venga a nosotros tu reino;
hágase tu voluntad en la tierra
como en el cielo.
Danos hoy nuestro pan de cada día;
perdona nuestras ofensas
como también nosotros perdonamos
a los que nos ofenden;
no nos dejes caer en la tentación
y líbranos del mal.
Amén.

Avemaría

Dios te salve, María;
llena eres de gracia;
el Señor es contigo;
bendita tú eres entre todas las mujeres,
y bendito es el fruto de tu vientre, Jesús.
Santa María, Madre de Dios,
ruega por nosotros, pecadores,
ahora y en la hora de nuestra muerte.
Amén.

Dirección editorial
Raquel López Varela
Coordinación editorial
Ana María García Alonso
Maquetación
Cristina A. Rejas Manzanera
Diseño de cubierta
Francisco A. Morais

© Ana Galán, del texto
© Núria Feijoó, de la ilustración
© EDITORIAL EVEREST, S. A.
Carretera León - La Coruña, km. 5 LEÓN
ISBN: 84-441-4804-5
Depósito Legal: LE. 550-2012
Printed in Spain - Impreso en España
EDITORIAL EVERGRÁFICAS, S. L.
Carretera León - La Coruña, km. 5
LEÓN (España)
Atención al cliente: 902 123 400

Conoce nuestros productos en esta página, danos tu opinión y
descárgate gratis nuestro catálogo.

www.everest.es

You've Got SPIRIT!

Cheers, Chants, Tips, and Tricks Every Cheerleader Needs to Know

SARA R. HUNT

illustrations by LISA PERRETT

M
Millbrook Press • Minneapolis

FOR MY FAMILY—
MY BIGGEST
CHEERLEADERS!
—S.R.H.

A special thank you to Josette Scheer, University of Wisconsin Spirit Director, for her enthusiasm and willingness to review the book prior to publication. Special thanks also to Kelsey Hunt (my co-captain), Phoebe Gilbert (cheer bows), and the AHS cheerleaders for their inspiration.

This book provides general information on cheerleading. It is not intended to serve as a step-by-step guide to specific cheerleading moves or to replace the instruction provided by a coach. Please use caution and common sense when attempting any cheerleading moves. Consult with a doctor or other health professional before beginning any exercise program. See the safety tips on page 14 for more information.

Milbrook Press
A division of Lerner Publishing Group, Inc.
241 First Avenue North
Minneapolis, MN 55401 U.S.A.

Website address: www.lernerbooks.com

Library of Congress Cataloging-in-Publication Data

Hunt, Sara R.
    You've got spirit! : cheers, chants, tips, and tricks every cheerleader needs to
  know / by Sara R. Hunt.
       p.   cm.
      ISBN 978–0–7613–8634–6 (lib. bdg. : alk. paper)
      1. Cheerleading—Juvenile literature. I. Title.
  LB3635.H86 2013
  791.6'4—dc23   2012020916

Manufactured in the United States of America
1 – DP – 12/31/12

The Sport of CHEERLEADING

TWO, FOUR, SIX, EIGHT, CHEERLEADING IS REALLY GREAT!

1958

Cheerleading has come a long way since it first began more than one hundred years ago. While it started as an activity meant to boost school spirit, it's now a competitive sport popular with girls and boys of all ages.

Cheerleaders need to have strength, athleticism and, of course, lots of spirit! Today cheerleading is popular in many countries all around the world.

This book will tell you what a cheerleader needs to know about everything from stunts and jumps to cheers and chants. Whether you love to cheer or love to watch, you'll learn what it takes to be a great cheerleader. Plus, get tips about tryouts; cheer gear; healthy snacks; and all-star nail, skin, and hair care.

Let's jump right into the sport of cheerleading!

How It All Began

The first cheerleaders were male "pep club" members who organized chants at college football games in the 1800s. Women did not become members of college cheerleading squads until the 1920s. High school cheerleading became popular during the 1950s. Then, during the 1970s,

DID YOU KNOW? THERE ARE ABOUT 3 MILLION CHEERLEADERS IN THE UNITED STATES!

1924

more difficult skills such as tumbling and stunting were included along with the chants. In the 1980s and the 1990s, cheerleading expanded to include a wide range of age and skill levels. Today cheerleaders are athletes, just like members of a soccer, track, tennis, or football team.

Why Cheer?

Cheerleading is a lot of fun, but that's just the beginning of the benefits! Cheerleaders learn a lot of important skills that will help them throughout their lives. They learn to be good sports and confident role models. They also learn how to manage their time, cooperate as part of a team, and work hard for something they believe in. Building friendships with their teammates is another bonus!

Some people who don't know a lot about cheerleading have the wrong impression of cheerleaders. They think cheerleadering is not very hard and that cheerleaders are not very smart. This is mainly because of the way cheerleaders have been shown in the movies and on TV. The truth is that cheerleaders get good grades and spend hours every week at practice. Many of them also participate in other sports, and a lot of them are really involved in their schools and communities.

Today

Cheerleading is more hard work and dedication than glitter and glamour. Cheerleading squads put in a lot of time and effort to practice, practice, practice until their performance shines!

Competition vs. Sideline

There are two main types of cheerleading. When you first think of cheerleading, you might picture the sideline cheerleaders you see at sporting events. The main goal of **sideline cheerleading** is to increase support for a sports team and keep the crowd excited at games. All the cheerleaders usually attend the same school or participate in a local youth recreation league. The season for sideline cheerleaders is usually the same as the season they are cheering for (such as football in the fall or basketball in the winter). Practices can be two to three hours long and as often as three or four times a week. In addition to cheering at sporting events, many sideline squads also perform in competitions with other cheer squads in their league.

Competition cheerleading (also known as All-Star) is a competitive sport. Squads perform a two-minute, 30-second routine that may include tumbling, stunts, pyramids, dance, and cheer segments. Judges watch the

performances and give each segment a score. The team with the highest combined score wins! There are local, regional, national, and worldwide competitions.

All-Star cheerleading teams often practice year-round. The cheerleaders are not required to be from the same school or area. They belong to a specific cheer gym, or club. In many cases, the skills needed for competition are much more difficult than those required for sideline cheerleading. Competitive cheering requires a huge time commitment. It takes the same dedication of time and effort as a club soccer team or a traveling baseball team. Between practices and competitions, competitive cheerleaders may spend up to 20 hours a week cheering.

Put It All Together

Cheerleaders don't just cheer. They jump, tumble, dance, and stunt too. Here is a breakdown of these important skills.

Cheering is when team members use sharp, coordinated motions while they chant a cheer for their team.

Jumping is exactly what it sounds like! Cheerleaders have many different arm and leg positions for jumps.

Tumbling includes basic skills like forward rolls and cartwheels and more advanced gymnastics skills such as round-offs, back handsprings, and back tucks.

Dancing features choreographed, high-energy dance moves done to music.

Stunting involves one or more cheerleaders lifting and holding another cheerleader in the air.

CHEER +
LEADER =
CHEERLEADER

Join the Squad!

There are many different age groups, divisions, and levels for competitive cheerleading. This helps make sure each team competes against others of the same age and skill level. Age groups range from mini (ages 8 and under) to youth (11 and under), junior (14 and under), and senior (18 and under). Teams can be either all-girl or coed (including boys and girls). Teams might range in size from five or six members to more than 30! The levels range from 1 to 6, with level 1 being the entry level and level 6 being the most difficult. Levels are based on skill, not on age, so sometimes younger cheerleaders compete at higher levels than older ones.

CHEER GEAR

Every sport has its own special gear and uniforms, and cheerleading is no different. Here are the essentials.

Shell Top

This is the top part of the uniform. It usually has the team name or initials on the front.

Skirt

This is the bottom part of the uniform. (Boys wear pants.) Cheer skirts usually have contrasting stripes or insets on the side to match the top.

Cheer Shoes

This is the one item you will wear for practice every day as well as for competitions and performances. Most cheerleading shoes are white and come with changeable color inserts that go in special panels on the sides. Look for a shoe that is as lightweight as possible but still offers comfort, support, and durability. Some cheer shoes have extra features that are helpful for stunting or tumbling such as finger grips or grooves, flexibility, shock absorption, or ankle support. Many sporting goods stores sell cheer shoes, and you can also find them online.

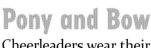

Pony and Bow

Cheerleaders wear their hair up for practice as well as for competition and games. Your coach may tell you a specific hairstyle to wear so that the whole team looks uniform.

Tie off your ponytail with a hair bow. Some teams have a special bow for competitions.

Think of your ponytail as an extra pom on the top of your head. Of course, it's OK if you have short hair! See tips on page 41.

Poms

Cheerleaders get the crowd excited with colorful poms. Poms come in different sizes, colors, and styles. They can have solid, two-color, or three-color plastic streamers. Metallic poms are also popular for performances. Poms are available with a grasp handle on the end or a baton handle (in the center). Sizes range from 4 to 10 inches (10 to 25 centimeters) in diameter.

NOTE: Fan poms, known as rooter poms or shakers, are also available. They usually have a long handle and are meant for fans to shake in the stands.

Cheer Briefs

You wear them under your skirt so that when you are tumbling or stunting your underwear doesn't show. These are sometimes called spankies, trunks, lollies, or bloomers.

Megaphone

Cheerleaders use a megaphone to project their voices. It helps make them louder so that the fans in the stands can hear them!

Anklet Socks

To look its best, your team will want to match—all the way down to the socks! Find out what your team is wearing so you are sure to have the right socks. A popular choice is white low or no-show anklet socks.

Cheer Bag

Keep your cheer bag stocked so you're always ready when it's time to go to practice, competitions, or games. Keep your poms, warm-ups, and body liner in your bag at all times. If you are a sideline cheerleader, be sure you are prepared for the weather on game day. A rain poncho or warm-up can save the day if the weather suddenly changes.

It is also a good idea to keep extra hair ties, socks, elastic bandages, deodorant, and pads or tampons (if you use them) in your bag. If you have extra briefs and spare cheer shoes, throw those in too!

Warm-ups

Warm-ups keep cheerleaders warm and also help identify them as part of the same team. You may need these for cooler weather, traveling, and before and after competitions.

Bodysuit or Body liner

The bodysuit (or body liner) is the shirt that you wear under your shell for a long-sleeve look (or warmth). Available in a rainbow of colors—even metallic—bodysuits usually have a mock turtleneck. Some bodysuits are cropped at the midriff to be worn under two-piece uniforms. Others are like a leotard on the bottom so you don't have to worry about keeping them tucked in.

SEE WWW.LERNERESOURCE.COM TO FIND A GEAR LIST FOR CHEER CAMP TOO!

TRAINING TIPS

Cheerleading requires endurance, strength, flexibility, and balance. How can you train to be a good cheerleader? These are all things you can work on.

Endurance

Endurance refers to how long you can exercise without stopping. To build endurance, try to do something that gets your heart beating faster for at least an hour, five times per week. You can work on endurance at practice or on your own. At practice, you might do your competition routine three or more times in a row without stopping.

See the list below for some other activities you can do to get your heart pumping when you don't have practice.

- Running
- Rollerblading
- Jumping rope
- Zumba or other dance classes
- Walking
- Biking
- Hiking
- Swimming

Strength

Some athletes lift weights. Cheerleaders lift people! Lifting another cheerleader in a stunt or controlling your body in tumbling requires a lot of strength. All cheerleaders should have a strong core (back and stomach muscles). Arm and leg muscles are also important if you'll be tumbling or doing stunts. But you don't need to lift weights to strengthen your muscles. You can use your own body weight to build strength with exercises such as push-ups, squats, and lunges. Be careful not to overdo it, though. Take one day off between strength training sessions so your muscles can rest and recover.

Flexibility

Flexibility is important for performing jumps and stunts properly. Stretching should also be part of your routine during practice. To improve flexibility, try to stretch every day. You can even stretch while watching TV or doing your homework.

Before you stretch, do a five- to ten-minute warm-up. (You can run in place, jump rope, or just dance around.) Warm muscles stretch more easily than cold muscles. You should stretch far enough to feel it but not so far that you're in a lot of pain. Hold each stretch for 30 to 60 seconds without bouncing. Repeat every stretch two to three times. Improving flexibility takes a while, so don't expect to see changes right away. Your muscles will become more and more flexible over time.

Balance

Balance is key for all cheerleaders. To improve your balance, practice your stunting poses on the ground. Hold each position for at least 30 seconds. To add an extra challenge, try doing your poses on something wobbly. You can use a wobble board or wobble cushion (special products meant to help improve balance) or just take a cushion off your couch.

NOTE: For co-ed or partner stunting, it is important for the flyer to stay tight and allow the base to balance the stunt. If both are balancing, they will throw each other off and cause the stunt to fall!

Yoga Class

Doing this basic yoga pose can help you improve your balance.

TREE POSE

While you hold this pose, imagine that your standing leg is the trunk of a tree, firmly planted into the ground and that your arms are the tree's branches.

1. Start by standing tall with your feet together and your arms at your sides.
2. Breathe in, shifting your weight onto one leg.
3. As you breathe out, bring your other foot up and turn that knee out to the side. Rest that foot as high as you can on the other leg. If you lose your balance, move slowly back into position.
4. Try raising your hands straight out from your sides. If you feel balanced, inhale and reach your hands all the way up so that your palms meet overhead.

Hold the position for a count of ten while you continue breathing slowly. As you breathe out, return your lifted foot to the floor. Repeat on the other side.

PLAY iT SAFE

Like all sports, cheerleading has a certain risk of injury. But you can do a lot to stay safe.

SAFETY RULES

Always warm up and stretch before each practice or competition.

Tell your coach about any medical conditions that you have. This helps your coach know what to look for in case of an emergency. It also helps your coach know what expectations or goals are right for you.

Don't talk when the coach is giving instructions or demonstrating.

Don't chew gum or eat candy during practices or competitions.

Wear proper clothes and shoes at all times.

Remove all jewelry, including earrings, during practices and competitions.

Practice stunts and tumbling only when a coach is watching. (No exceptions!)

Wear proper safety equipment for weak ankles, knees, or wrists.

Stay focused. Don't run or goof around during practices or competitions.

Be sure to let your coach know if you feel too tired or if something hurts.

If you think you might be injured, tell your coach or another adult right away!

Do not attempt any moves that are beyond your ability or have not been approved by your coach.

Make sure your coach is trained or certified in cheerleading safety.

Only perform stunts and tumbling on safe surfaces, such as landing mats on foam floors or spring-loaded floors.

Motions and Emotions

Cheerleading is all about showing spirit. The best way to do that is with your motions (arm positions and body movements), emotions (facial expressions and smile), and your voice.

Snap to It

Cheer moves are very tight and straight. When you clap, keep your arms in front of you. Keep your hands at mouth or nose height on the clap. Don't let your hands go past your shoulders on the release. To learn that tight, snappy cheerleader clap, take turns with a partner. Have your partner put her hands on your shoulders while you practice clapping in the space in between her arms.

GIVE ME A C FOR COMMITMENT

Cheerleading is a team sport. When one person is absent, the whole team suffers and can't practice the routine. Make a commitment to be at all practices, ready to do your best!

CHEER ABCs

ARM MOTION ABCs

High V

Low V

T

Broken T

Punch

Bow and Arrow

Touchdown

Low Touchdown

16

Right Diagonal

Left Diagonal

Right L

Left L

Right K

Left K

Candlesticks

Buckets

Daggers

Spirit Fingers

Cheerleaders don't always have poms in their hands. An iconic cheerleader motion is the "spirit fingers." Similar to "jazz hands" for a dancer, spirit fingers are a quick, controlled wiggle of the fingers on stiff hands with straight, outstretched arms (usually in a high V). Try wiggling your fingers without moving your arms or hands. Use your spirit fingers to rev up the crowd.

Facials

In cheerleading, the term *facials* doesn't have anything to do with cucumber masks or oatmeal scrubs. Facials refer to the expressions on your face while cheering. Since you will look very small from the stands where the crowd is watching from, you want to make your facial expressions larger than life.

Excessive facials are more common in competitive cheerleading, where you really want to impress the judges. Play it up with big smiles, winks, or by opening your eyes wide and shaking your head either up and down or side to side—with a pop. Exaggerating your facial expressions might feel funny to do at first, but once you get the hang of it, it's fun. Try practicing in the mirror until you're comfortable showing your stuff at practice!

Got Spirit? Let's Hear It!

There is no such thing as "inside voices" in cheerleading. To be heard, you need to use your loudest, clearest CHEER voice. And since you will often be jumping, dancing, stunting, and tumbling at the same time as you're cheering, you'll need good lung control too. This is a lot harder than it sounds. To get used to it, your coach will have you practice your routines and cheers together—a lot—because that will help you to be able to do both at the same time. The better you know the moves, the less you'll have to think about them and the more likely you are to remember and perform the words.

Save your sweet singsong voice for music class. For cheers, try to say each syllable loudly and clearly. In other words, no mumbling!

If you just try to scream or yell as loud as you can, you'll end up with a sore throat (and you'll never make it through a game)! Instead, use your stomach muscles to project your voice. To practice this, lie on your back and do your cheers with your hands on your stomach. Make sure that when you cheer, you feel your belly move. This will help you learn to yell from your belly rather than your throat.

Stunts and Jumps

Stunting

One of the most popular parts of cheer performances is the stunting. Based on your individual strengths and skills, your coach will find the stunt position that suits you best.

Stunt Positions

Top or Flyer Cheerleaders who are on top of a stunt or in a flying position when coming out of a stunt. Flyers must remember to always go up fast, stay tight, and keep their legs straight. They are usually the smallest—and bravest—members of the team.

Bases Cheerleaders who lift, toss, hold, and catch the flyers. Lifting should always be done with the legs and not with the back. Bases must stay as still as possible while performing a stationary stunt.

Spotters Cheerleaders who assist in the stunt by lifting, bracing, and catching. Spotters can be in the front and back if necessary. They are responsible for the stunt count, which helps everyone coordinate their movements so the stunt goes smoothly.

Cheerleading is like any team sport. Coaches will make decisions based on what's best for the team as a whole rather than what will benefit one squad member. If you have any questions about your coaches' decisions, just ask!

All stunting should be supervised by a coach.
Stunting should only be done after the basic cheerleading skills are mastered.
No horseplay or joking during practice—this can result in serious injury.

Stunt in Style

Here are some of the most popular cheerleading stunts.

Elevator An elevator, also known as a prep or half, is the most basic stunt in cheerleading. It is a very important skill for every team to learn because it serves as the foundation for all other stunts. It also teaches proper timing, body position, and technique. Once mastered, the elevator can lead to other, more difficult skills such as an extension or a liberty.

Liberty

Extension

STICK IT!
TO STICK A STUNT MEANS TO HOLD THE STUNT WITHOUT FALLING.

21

Heel Stretch

Scale

Pyramid

Cupie

Scorpion

Arabesque

GIVE ME AN
A
FOR
ATTITUDE

Cheerleaders should display a positive attitude at all times. Always listen to what your coach asks you to do and remember— cheerleading is a team sport. What is best for the team is best for you!

CHEER ABCs

Jumping

All cheer jumps are made up of four basic steps. Each jump is done in eight counts. Before the jump, someone will call off "5, 6, 7, 8."

The Prep (1, 2): This is the preparation. Keep your body tight with your legs together. Start with your hands at your sides. A common prep is a clasp on count 1. A clasp is like a clap but with your hands cupped together tightly. Hold the clasp on count 2.

The Lift (3, 4): Throw your arms into high V on count 3 as you rise up on tiptoes. Hold on count 4.

The Jump (5, 6): Build momentum by swinging your arms down and crossing them in front of your body on count 5 as you bend your knees to prepare for takeoff. Your arms and legs should hit the jump position on count 6. Keep your chest and head up high during the jump. The position of your arms and legs will depend on which jump you are doing.

The Landing (7, 8): You're not done yet! This is the last thing the audience will see, so stay tight. Be sure to snap your legs down into position and try to land with your feet and your knees together on count 7. Remember to bend your knees to absorb the landing and keep your shoulders slightly forward to maintain balance. To finish, snap back and stand up straight (your coach might call this "clean") with your head held high on count 8. Now you're ready for the next jump or skill.

Remember to stretch your back, arm, leg, and stomach muscles before doing cheer jumps. Learn the proper way to do a cheer jump, and use the correct form to help prevent injury.

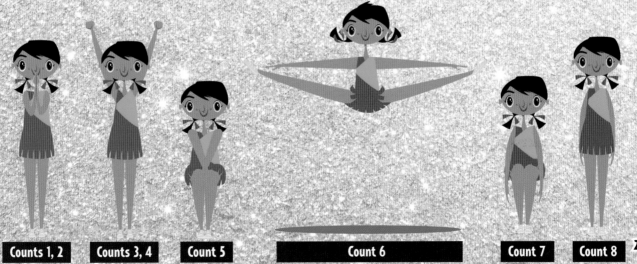

Counts 1, 2   Counts 3, 4   Count 5   Count 6   Count 7   Count 8

JUMP! JUMP! JUMP!

Here are the most common cheer jumps.

Side Hurdler

Pike

Toe Touch or Straddle Jump

This is the most popular cheer jump. Despite its name, you don't actually touch your toes during a toe touch. Keep your chest up and reach out past your toes, in front of your legs. Keep your back straight and bring your legs up to you.

Spread Eagle

Herkie

This jump was named after Lawrence "Herkie" Herkimer, a pioneer in the sport of cheerleading who invented this jump. He also patented the pom-pom!

Tuck

Jump Drills

To practice a specific jump, do five jumps in a row without a prep or pause in between. Land with your knees slightly bent and immediately spring back up into another jump. Repetition will work the muscles used for that jump and improve your form.

On Your Toes

Many cheerleaders think that using the whole foot to spring off the ground will make them jump higher. But jumping off the balls of your feet will actually make your jumps higher!

T-T-TRYOUTS

Not all cheer teams have an official tryout. Some just require that you attend regular practices and competitions, work hard, and be a good teammate. If you do have to try out for a spot on the squad, here are some suggestions.

Details

Find out this information in advance so that you are prepared for the big day!

Where tryouts will be
(be sure you know where that is!)

When you need to be there
(get there early!)

What you need to wear
(make sure it's ready and clean the night before)

If there's anything you need to bring or paperwork you need to fill out
(permission slips, doctor forms, insurance cards, waivers, or payments that your parents need to have ready)

What you'll be expected to do at tryouts
(what skills or cheers you will be evaluated on)

If tryouts are held over a series of practices, keep in mind that the coach is evaluating you the entire time, not just during the official tryout at the end. Keep a positive attitude and work hard every day of the tryout period.

Practice, Practice, Practice!

The more you practice your routine, the greater chance that your muscle memory will carry you through the tryout. Your body will remember what to do even if your brain doesn't!

Listen Up

Believe it or not, but one of the most important skills that cheer coaches are looking for is being a good listener. Be sure you listen to everything that is taught the whole time (and don't talk to friends when you should be listening). Try your best to do what you've been asked to do. Showing the coach that you're a good listener and that you can learn a new cheer, skill, or stunt will go very far in earning extra points on your tryout score sheet.

Be Flexible

If you are trying out for a cheer team that performs stunts, be flexible about which stunt group or partner you work with. As a member of a team, you need to be able to work with many people—not just your best cheer pal. Showing the coach that you're willing to work with others will also increase your chance of being selected.

Be Proud

If you're good at a particular skill, be proud of it! If you perform your signature skill at the appropriate time (not when you just want to show off), it shows confidence and you won't come off as being braggy. Be sure you compliment other girls on their skills too!

The Night Before

It's probably not a good idea to have a sleepover the night before tryouts! Have a good dinner, relax at home, and get to bed early. Even though you're excited about tryouts, try not to think too much about them—you don't want your excitement to turn into worry. Just close your eyes and imagine yourself doing a great job!

Look Your Best

If you want to be selected as a cheerleader, be sure you look the part. Come to tryouts dressed as if it were a game or competition, with

hair up and the appropriate gear. Remember, you are trying out for a position to represent a school, cheer gym, or club. Wear team colors!

Ready? OK!

Just before your turn, stay calm. Close your eyes and take a deep breath. Breathe in through your nose, and exhale slowly from your mouth. Stand up tall with your shoulders back—be strong! Now's your chance to shine.

When your name is called, put on a big smile and show your stuff! If you make a mistake, keep going. Don't draw attention to it by getting flustered. Show that you are confident enough not to let a mistake throw you off.

What If You Don't Make It?

If you really want to be a cheerleader and you don't make the team, it can be very disappointing. But don't give up! There might be other ways to be involved with the team or other ways to be involved with cheer. Ask the coach if there are things you can improve and try out again the next time tryouts are held. If it was a school team you didn't make, see if you can join a club cheer team at a local gym instead. If you don't make a local club team, you could try out for a school or rec team.

GIVE ME AN R FOR RESPECT

Cheerleaders should maintain respect for themselves, teammates, coaches, opponents, and the audience at all times. It's never OK to taunt, brag, or use suggestive expressions or inappropriate gestures.

HEALTHY U

Taking good care of yourself will help you look and feel your best both on and off the mat or field!

Nails

Keep fingernails neat and trimmed. Even a little length can scratch you or a teammate during stunting.

Smile

A smile is one of a cheerleader's most important features, so be sure to take good care of yours! Brush and floss regularly to keep your teeth healthy. Use lip balm to keep your lips from chapping.

Skin

If you are old enough to shave your legs, you'll want to make an extra effort to stay on top of it. If you're a flyer, your stunt group will thank you! Flyers should also avoid using lotion on their arms and legs, especially right before cheerleading. Smooth skin can make you extra slippery, and it will make it difficult for bases and back spotters to get a good grip on you. Back spotters and bases should avoid using lotion on their hands for the same reason.

Hair Care

Before you shower, brush your hair to loosen dirt and tangles. Once you're in the shower, wet hair thoroughly. Gently work the shampoo into your scalp and through your hair. Don't pile hair on top of your head and scrub it—that will create tangles. Tilt your head back and rinse with warm water in the direction your hair grows. Then apply conditioner, making sure you work it through your hair. Rinse again.

After you shower, blot—don't rub—your hair with a towel. Comb wet hair before drying it instead of brushing it. Hair dryers are great when you're running late, but too much heat can damage your hair. Let your hair air dry whenever possible. If you do use a dryer, use a warm or cool setting—not hot. And if you feel like you must straighten your hair with a flat iron, be sure to use products to protect your hair from heat damage.

Use a comb to gently work through tangles, starting at the ends and working up. If you wear your hair up, be sure to use real hair ties—not rubber bands—and pull them out gently to avoid breaking your hair.

Spirit Fingers

Try this recipe for a spa manicure you can mix up yourself. When you're done, paint your nails with clear or white polish. For game day, use team colors!

1. Hand scrub—pour a small amount of fine sea salt into the palm of your hand and mix with olive oil. Rub mixture all over your hands. Rinse with warm water and dry with a clean towel.
2. Soak—remove nail polish and soak fingertips in a bowl with 1 cup warm milk and 1 tablespoon lemon juice for 5 to 10 minutes. Rinse off and dry.
3. Massage—dab baby oil or lotion into your cuticle area. Rub in.

SNAPPY SNACKS

Eat a well-balanced diet to fuel your body for cheerleading. Be sure to eat a healthy breakfast, lunch, and dinner every day. To keep your energy level up, keep healthy snacks on hand as well. Here are some great snacks for before, during, or after cheer practice. Fruits and veggies make simple, all-natural, grab-and-go snacks!

Fruits

Apple slices
Bananas
Berries (blueberries, strawberries, raspberries)
Grapes

Fruit Dip

For a little something sweet, dip fruit in whipped topping. Or try one of the yummy dip recipes below.

Sugar 'n' Spice Fruit Dip

Mix 4 tablespoons packed brown sugar with $\frac{1}{8}$ teaspoon cinnamon and a dash of nutmeg. Stir sugar and spices into 2 cups thawed whipped topping. Store in the refrigerator until ready to serve.

Nutty Fruit Dip

Mix together 1 cup low-fat vanilla yogurt, 3 tablespoons peanut butter, and 1 tablespoon unsweetened cocoa powder in a bowl.

Veggies

Avocado
Broccoli
Carrots
Celery
Red and green bell peppers

Tip: For extra flavor, dip veggies in ranch dressing or hummus.

Simple Snack Recipes

Pear Salad

Slice pears in half (or use pear halves from a can). Arrange half of a pear on a plate, scoop low-fat cottage cheese into the center, and top with shredded cheddar cheese.

Frozen Chocolate-Covered Bananas

Peel a banana, cut it in half, and freeze for 2 hours on a piece of wax paper. Roll frozen bananas in melted chocolate, then in chopped nuts or ice cream sprinkles, and freeze till set. Yum!

Banana Graham

Spread a graham cracker with chocolate hazelnut spread and top with banana slices.

DID YOU KNOW? BANANAS HAVE POTASSIUM, WHICH CAN HELP PREVENT CRAMPING, SO THEY'RE A GOOD BEFORE-EXERCISE SNACK.

33

Mock Apple Pie

Pour ½ cup graham cracker crumbs into a small bowl. Add a spoonful of applesauce and top off with a dollop of whipped topping.

Make-Believe Cheesecake

Spread a small amount of cream cheese and strawberry jam between graham crackers for a cheesecake-inspired snack.

Fruit 'n' Juice Pops

½ cup fruit (diced strawberries, pineapple, or blueberries)
2 cups of 100 percent fruit juice (orange, pineapple, or mango juice)

Fill freezer-pop molds three-quarters full with fruit juice. Add pieces of fruit to each mold. Freeze 8 hours. Makes 6 to 8 pops.

Celery Boats

Spread 1 tablespoon cream cheese, pineapple cream cheese, peanut butter, or pimento cheese spread on a celery stick. Dot with raisins or sliced green olives.

Watermelon Sorbet

Put 4 cups cubed seedless watermelon, ½ cup sugar, and 1 tablespoon lemon or lime juice in a food processor or blender. Blend until smooth. Pour mixture into a shallow dish and freeze for 1 hour. Flake with a fork and freeze until firm (2 more hours). Flake mixture again and serve in cups.

FIND LOTS MORE GREAT SNACK IDEAS AT WWW.LERNERESOURCE.COM!

Get Crafty

It's fun to spread cheer by making a spirit gift for a teammate or coach. These are also fun ideas for crafts and activities at a cheer-themed party.

Water Break

Decorate a water bottle with three-dimensional craft paint. Fill it with special treats like candy, anklets, nail polish, hair ties, and other small items. Tie it with a big ribbon bow.

You could also paint a water bottle with acrylic craft paint, completely covering it. Then attach paper decorations with Mod Podge. Finally, coat everything with a layer of Mod Podge and let dry.

Sleeping Beauty

Decorate a spare pillow sham or pillowcase with puff paint. Write messages like "All-Star Cheerleader Sleeps Here!" or "Cheerleaders Need Their Beauty Sleep!" or "Eat. Sleep. Cheer. (Repeat!)."

Square Up

Paint a square canvas from the craft store with craft paint. Let dry. Use a white paint pen to write a message like "If it's in your heart, it shows in your spirit!" or "It's not whether you win or lose, it's how LOUD you cheer!" to cheer up a teammate or coach. Decorate with dots, swirls, and squiggles.

Gift Card Tree

To thank your coach at the end of the season, invite teammates to participate in this fun group gift! Teammates bring a gift card of their choice (any amount). Use floral inserts (available at craft stores) to put the cards on a potted plant.

It's a Snap

This is a great gift idea for a coach. Decorate a large jar and write the word *Snaps* with a marker or a paint pen on the cover or the side. Anytime a teammate does a good job at practice or learns a new skill, cheer her on with a short note that you place into the jar. Once a week at practice, teammates read the notes and the whole team celebrates the accomplishments by snapping their fingers!

Spirit Poppers

Turn a toilet paper tube into a spirit cracker. Fill an empty tube with goodies (ponytail holders and hair clips, nail polish and nail clippers, mini lotion and shampoo, snacks, etc.). Wrap the tube in tissue paper and secure with tape. Making sure to keep contents inside, tie the ends of the tissue paper with ribbon, pipe cleaners, or pom-pom strips.

Flower Girls

Make corsages for coaches or teammates for a special occasion. Trim fresh carnations, leaving about 2 inches (5 cm) of the stem attached. Wrap the stem with floral wire and cover with floral tape. Attach a flower to your top using two straight pins with pearls on the ends. (The wire, the tape, and the pins can all be found at craft stores.)

Goody Bag

Decorate a standard pillowcase with fleece cutouts (letters, stars, megaphones) attached with craft glue. Use a long ribbon to tie the bag closed. Use it as an overnight bag for your next cheer sleepover.

GIVE ME AN F FOR FRIENDSHIP

Your teammates will be among your very best friends! You will spend hours together practicing, working toward a common goal, and experiencing success (and sometimes setbacks) together.

CHEER ABCs

CHEER BOWS AND MORE

Turn ribbon, glue, and wire into an all-star cheer bow! Some steps require a hot glue gun, so you will need an adult to help you.

For each bow, you will need:
1 yard (1 meter) of 2-inch (5 cm) wide ribbon
1 yard (1 m) of 1.5-inch (3.8 cm) wide ribbon
 in a coordinating color
2 yards (1.8 m) narrow trim ribbon
5 inches (12.5 cm) of ribbon for the center
Premium craft and fabric glue (like Sobo)
5 inches (12.5 cm) of 20-gauge craft or
 jewelry wire
Hot glue gun
Ponytail holder
Fray Check
Fabric paint pen (optional)

1. Run three strips of glue down the 2-inch ribbon and set the 1.5-inch ribbon on top. Run a single strip of glue down each side of the 1.5-inch ribbon. Attach satin trim ribbon to the glue. When the glue dries, the bow will be stiff.
2. To create the bow shape, make a large loop, like a cursive lowercase *l*. Bring the back of the top of the loop behind the spot where the ribbons cross. Pinch tightly in the center. Shape into a bow and secure by wrapping several times with a length of wire.
3. Have an adult hot glue the knot part to the front of the bow, and place the short piece of ribbon over the glue dot with the tails extending above and below the bow.
4. Flip the bow over, put on another drop of hot glue, and attach a ponytail holder.
5. Wrap the bottom tail of the middle ribbon over the ponytail holder, trim any excess, and have an adult hot glue it down. Then fold over the top tail, trim excess (leaving just enough to turn under the raw edge), and hot glue it down.
6. To finish, trim the ribbon tails into a V shape and apply a little Fray Check to the ends so they don't unravel. Now you can decorate your new bow with the fabric paint pen, if desired!

CAN'T GET ENOUGH OF POM-POMS? Here are three cute ideas!

Pom-Pom Ponytail Holder
Cut about nine 6-inch (15 cm) pieces of ribbon (organdy, grosgrain, or satin). Tie each ribbon piece tightly around a hair elastic so all the ends bunch up to form a pom.

Shoe Poms
Hold the end of a piece of yarn with your left thumb pressed against your left palm. Loosely wrap the yarn around your other fingers 30 times. Slip the yarn off. Repeat with a different color. Stack the two colors of yarn. Tie one long piece of yarn around the middle in a tight double knot. Snip the loops open and fluff. Tie the loose long piece in a double knot around a shoelace.

The Wave
Make mini poms (see shoe poms left), and stitch or glue them to the fingertips of a pair of inexpensive gloves. Wear them to games to keep your hands warm, and wiggle your fingers for spirit!

PERFECT PONYTAIL

Cheerleaders use their hair like an extra pom for emphasis and style. The go-to hairstyle for cheerleaders is the ponytail because it keeps hair out of your face and off your shoulders so it won't get tangled in a stunt.

Before

Wash and shampoo your hair. (A perfect ponytail requires perfectly clean hair.) Slightly damp hair holds in shorter layers as the hair dries.

Straight hair works best for a ponytail, so blow-dry your hair straight with a blow-dryer that has a concentrator attachment. Leave hair a little damp. For naturally wavy or curly hair, apply straightening balm or gel to damp strands.

Use a comb with a tail to make a neat, straight part. Most cheerleaders use a center part, but sometimes a side or angled part can add a dramatic effect (if your coach is OK with it). For a smooth look, comb hair straight back without a part at all.

Step-by-Step

1. Put your fingers at the crown of your head.
2. Gather a large section of hair from the top of your head, about 3 inches (7.5 cm) wide by 2 inches (5 cm) deep.

3. Tease the underside to give it extra volume.
4. Run your hairbrush over this section lightly.
5. Pull hair into a ponytail just above the middle point at the back of your head.
6. Secure with a ponytail elastic.
7. Finish with medium hold hairspray on the sides and back of the hair.

Tips

Hold your head back when pulling your hair up and fixing the elastic to avoid a "pouf" under your pony.

If your hair starts to look a bit dry or frizzy after a while, smooth strands with leave-in conditioner to keep it fresh and smooth.

GIVE ME AN
S
FOR
SPORTSMANSHIP

Cheering for your team is important, but remember to be respectful of the opposing team too. Always cheer on your team whether they win or lose.

CHEER ABCs

Short Stuff

Cheerleaders don't all have to have long hair. There are still ways to add some spirit to a short hairstyle. Use colorful clips to hold hair back on the sides, or add a hair bow to a barrette with hot glue to clip into short hair.

CHEERS AND CHANTS

Cheers

We got the beat, that Tigers* beat,
that Tigers* beat goes
(slap, slap, clap, clap, snap, snap, clap, clap,
slap, clap, snap, clap, slap, snap, clap).
*insert your team's name
....

PUMP up that spirit
So everyone can hear it.
Our team is on a mission,
and you know we're gonna WIN.
....

If you're from Westlake* and you're proud,
Stand up, say it loud.
Go BLACK*, Go WHITE.*
*insert your school's name and school colors
....

When we say Western*, you say Warriors*,
Western (Warriors), Western (Warriors).
When we say blue*, you say gold*,
Blue (gold), blue (gold).
When we say number, you say one,
Number (one), number (one).
*insert your school, team's name and colors

When we say go, you say fight.
When we say win, you say tonight.
When we say boogie, you say down.
Go (fight), win (tonight).
Boogie (down) all right, all right!
....

We're fired up with spirit,
So come on now let's hear it.
We'll do it, do it with lots of style.
Hey, hey, we say, everybody get wild!
....

Come on Mustangs*.
You can do it.
Let's SNAP to it!
*insert your team's name
....

G-G-O let me hear you go (go!).
That's right, unite.
Let me hear you fight (fight!).
W-I-N let me hear you win (win!).
Put it all together: go, fight, win!
....

Clap it high (clap).
Clap it low (clap).
Come on fans.
Go Rams* go.
*insert your team's name
....

Go, go get 'em, get 'em.
Go, go get 'em, get 'em.
Ooossh, ah, ooossh, ah,
Come on Patriots.*
You can do it.
Put a little power to it!
*insert your team's name

Football Cheers

Defense: When the other team has the ball. The main goal of the defense is to stop the other team from scoring. These are all good cheers for when your team is on defense.

Defense, it's up to you.
Guard your man.
Don't let him through.

....

Push 'em back.
Push 'em back.
Waaay back.

Push 'em back.
Pull 'em back.
Any way to get 'em back.

....

Offense: When your team has the ball. The main goal of the offense is to score points!

We want a Touchdown!

....

First and ten, let's do it again!

....

How about a touchdown.
How 'bout a score.
We have some, but we want more.

Basketball Cheers

She walked, she walked,
She traveled and got caught (uh-oh).

....

Want two,
Want two,
Want two from you.

Chants

B-E A-G-G-R-E-S-S-I-V-E.
Be aggressive, B-E aggressive!

....

S-C-O-R-E,
F-I-G-H-T,
W-I-N,
Score! Fight! Win!

....

S-P-I-R-I-T,
Got spirit? Let's hear it!

After the game

We are proud of you,
we are proud of you!

Glossary

aggressive: in sports, playing intensely with a lot of energy

athleticism: the qualities of being an athlete, including being muscular and having speed and endurance

attitude: a way of thinking or feeling

base: a cheerleader who lifts, tosses, holds, and catches the flyers

carnation: a common flower

commitment: a pledge or promise to do something

confidence: having belief in yourself and in your skills

emphasis: drawing extra attention to something

endurance: how long you can exercise without stopping

facials: the larger-than-life expressions used by cheerleaders

flexibility: the range of movement of joints and muscles

flyer: a cheerleader who is on top of a stunt or in a flying position when coming out of a stunt. Flyers are also called tops.

grosgrain: a type of ribbon that has a ribbed (bumpy) appearance

pom: also known as a pom-pom, these are big balls of streamers that are used by cheerleaders to get the crowd's attention

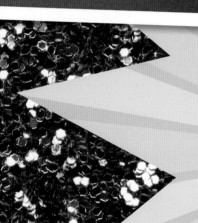

potassium: a chemical important for nutrition. It helps prevent muscles from cramping.

sportsmanship: playing fair and being respectful of your opponents

spotter: a cheerleader who assists in stunts by lifting, bracing, and catching

travel: in basketball, this is when one player moves illegally while holding the ball (such as taking too many steps without dribbling)

uniform: looking the same

yoga: a type of exercise that focuses on balance and strength

Further Reading and Websites

Fiction

Ambrose, Adrianne. *What I Learned from Being a Cheerleader.* Memphis: Bell Bridge Books, 2010.
This is a story about a girl who has to choose between her new friends and her old friends when she joins the cheerleading squad.

Evans, Zoe. *Confessions of a Wannabe Cheerleader.* New York: Simon Spotlight, 2011.
Maddie doesn't make it on to the cheerleading squad she expected to be on. Can she make the best of a bad situation?

Gassman, Julie. *Cheerleading Really Is a Sport.* Bloomington, MN: Stone Arch Books, 2011
A young girl has to find a way to prove to her older brother that she is an athlete too.

Krulik, Nancy. *Three Cheers for . . . Who?* New York: Grosset & Dunlap, 2011.
Part of the Katie Kazoo Switcheroo series, this book is about a spirit war between two different squads.

McCoy, Mimi. *The Accidental Cheerleader.* New York: Scholastic, 2006.
One friend talks another into trying out for the cheerleading squad.

Nonfiction

Crossingham, John. *Cheerleading in Action.* New York: Crabtree Books, 2003.
This book has information on basic skills, safety, and competitions.

Kenney, Karen Latchana. *Cool School Cheerleading.* Edina, MN: ABDO Pub. Co., 2011.
Find out all about after-school cheerleading, including how to get involved, build strong teams, and raise money.

Mullarkey, Lisa. *Cheerleading Spirit.* Berkeley Heights, NJ: Enslow Publishers, 2010.
This book tells readers what spirit is, how to express it, and how to inspire it. It includes information about forming a spirit club and holding a pep rally.

Wells, Don. *For the Love of Cheerleading.* New York: Weigl Publishers, 2005.
Read about cheerleading history, equipment, and superstars.

Websites

American Association of Cheerleading Coaches & Administrators
http://www.aacca.org
Find information about cheerleading safety and check out a list of coaches in your state who are certified by the AACCA.

America Needs Cheerleaders
http://www.americaneedscheerleaders.com
America Needs Cheerleaders is dedicated to promoting the positive contributions made by cheerleaders around the world. Its website includes a section on cheer history and links to additional cheer resources.

National Cheerleaders Association
http://www.nca.varsity.com
The site of the National Cheerleaders Association (NCA) is for parents and coaches as well as cheerleaders. It also has information about camps, competitions, and more.

Pop Warner Cheer and Dance
http://www.popwarner.com/cheer
This site has information about the Pop Warner Spirit Program, which provides kids an opportunity to perform in an organized, supervised, safety-oriented environment.

Universal Cheerleaders Association
http://www.uca.com
This is the official site of the Universal Cheerleaders Association (UCA). It offers information about safety, camps, and competitions.

U.S. All-Star Federation
http://www.usasf.net
The U.S. All-Star Federation focuses on All-Star cheerleading and dance. Its site includes a search tool for finding a member gym in your area.

LERNER SOURCE
GO BEYOND THE PRINTED BOOK. DOWNLOAD FUN, FREE BONUS CHEERLEADING INFO, HOW-TOS, AND QUIZZES FROM OUR WEBSITE, WWW.LERNERESOURCE.COM.

Index

Photo Acknowledgments

The images in this book are used with the permission of: glitter backgrounds © iStockphoto.com/The Power of Forever Photography, © iStockphoto.com/millionhope, © iStockphoto.com/Nastco, and © iStockphoto.com/Erika Croner; © Chris Curtis/Dreamstime.com, p. 3; © Stan Wayman/Time & Life Pictures/Getty Images, pp. 4–5; © Underwood & Underwood/CORBIS, p. 5 (top); © Zia Soleil/Iconica/Getty Images, pp. 5 (bottom), 22 (top left); © Sarah Rice/Star Ledger/CORBIS, p. 6 (top); AP Photo/Robert E. Klein, p. 6 (bottom); © Alin Dragulin/Alamy, p. 8; © Todd Strand/Independent Picture Service, pp. 9 (top), 13, 31 (trimmer), 36 (jar), 36 (scissors), 38–39 (all); © iStockphoto.com/Alex Slobodkin, p. 9 (bottom); © Karkas/Shutterstock.com, p. 10; AP Photo/Wilfredo Lee, p. 11 (top); © Monkeybusinessimages/Dreamstime.com, p. 11 (bottom left); © Peter Cade/Iconica/Getty Images, p. 11 (bottom right); © John Giustina/The Image Bank/Getty Images, p. 12 (top); © Image Source/Getty Images, pp. 12 (bottom), 22 (top right); © iStockphoto.com/Amy Myers, p. 15; © Andy Lyons/Getty Images, pp. 18 (top), 22 (bottom right); © Marla Brose/ZUMA Press/CORBIS, pp. 18 (bottom), 22 (center left); © Jose Luis Pelaez Inc/Blend Images/Getty Images, p. 19; © dmac/Alamy, p. 20; © Tony Anderson/Taxi/Getty Images, p. 21 (left); © Lance King/Getty Images, p. 21 (center); © H. Mark Weidman Photography/Alamy, p. 21 (right); © ZUMA Wire Service/Alamy, p. 22 (top center); © topdog images/Alamy, p. 22 (center right); © Rainier Ehrhardt/Augusta Chronicle/ZUMA Press, p. 26; © Ron Thompson/St. Petersburg Times/ZUMA Press, p. 27 (top); © Jim Mahoney/Dallas Morning News/CORBIS, p. 27 (bottom); © Tim Kitchen/Taxi/Getty Images, p. 28; © iStockphoto.com/bravo1954, p. 30; © Chiyacat/Dreamstime.com, p. 31 (brush and bands); © iStockphoto.com/Micah Young, p. 31 (balm); © Tatiana Volgutova/Dreamstime.com, p. 31 (comb); © iStockphoto.com/Dean Turner, p. 32 (pear); © iStockphoto.com/Eric Gevaert, p. 32 (peanut butter); © iStockphoto.com/Uyen Le, p. 32 (strawberries); © iStockphoto.com/pixhook, p. 33 (avocado); © iStockphoto.com/t_kimura, p. 33 (pepper); © iStockphoto.com/MorePixels, p. 33 (celery); © Vlue/Dreamstime.com, p. 33 (cracker); © atoss/Shutterstock.com, p. 33 (bananas); © iStockphoto.com/spxChrome, p. 34; © Macdsean/Dreamstime.com, p. 35 (bottle); © Design56/Dreamstime.com, p. 35 (glitter glue); © iStockphoto.com/aida ricciardiello caballero, p. 36 (paint); © Daniel Ryan Burch/Dreamstime.com, p. 37 (tape); © iStockphoto.com/tadamichi, p. 37 (carnation); © iStockphoto.com/Dean Bertoncelj, p. 41; © iStockphoto.com/DNY59, p. 43; AP Photo/Mel Evans, p. 44 (top left); © Science Faction/SuperStock, p. 44 (top right); © Saed Hindash/Star Ledger/CORBIS, p. 44 (center left); AP Photo/Connecticut Post, Christian Abraham, p. 44 (center right); © William Albert Allard/National Geographic/Getty Images, p. 44 (bottom left); © Big Cheese Special/Alamy, p. 44 (bottom right).

Front cover: © Lane Oatey/Blue Jean Images/Getty Images (top left); © David Davis/Dreamstime.com (top right); © Chris Curtis/Dreamstime.com (bottom left); © iStockphoto.com/Cindy Singleton (bottom right), © iStockphoto.com/The Power of Forever Photography (red and purple glitter); © iStockphoto.com/millionhope (gold glitter).
Back cover: © iStockphoto.com/The Power of Forever Photography (blue glitter); © iStockphoto.com/millionhope (gold glitter).

Main body text set in Constantia Regular 12/16.
Typeface provided by Microsoft.